T0078437

Hold on to God's Unchanging Hand and Pray!

God is Faithful

Dr. Z. S. L. Dinkins, ThD, DBA

WESTBOW
PRESS®
A DIVISION OF THOMAS NELSON
& ZONDERVAN

WestBow Press books may be ordered through booksellers or by contacting:

WestBow Press
A Division of Thomas Nelson & Zondervan
1663 Liberty Drive
Bloomington, IN 47403
www.westbowpress.com
844-714-3454

Scripture taken from the King James Version of the Bible.

ISBN: 978-1-6642-1768-3 (sc)
ISBN: 978-1-6642-1770-6 (hc)
ISBN: 978-1-6642-1769-0 (e)

Library of Congress Control Number: 2020925971

Print information available on the last page.

WestBow Press rev. date: 01/18/2021

O taste and see that the Lord is good: blessed
is the man that trusteth in him.

—PSALM 34:8

Pray without ceasing.

—1 THESSALONIANS 5:17

To all those who are struggling from day to day to push through a very difficult situation. God knows all about it. Hold on to God's unchanging hand and pray with thanksgiving in your heart, and then simply wait on the Lord. The Lord is nigh unto all those who call upon Him, and He heals the brokenhearted. Have faith in God and call on Him! He hears a sincere prayer. God is faithful.

> Jesus said, "I will not leave you comfortless:
> I will come to you" (John 14:18).

For God has established an everlasting covenant with His people. His Spirit says, "Come buy without money and price."

> Ho, everyone that thirsteth, come ye to the waters, and he that hath no money; come ye, buy, and eat; yea, come, buy wine and milk without money and without price. (Isaiah 55:1)

Hallelujah! Let go and let God fix it!

Give all praise, thanks, honor, and glory to God and to our Lord and Savior, Jesus Christ, the maker of heaven and earth!

Acknowledgments

I give thanks, praise, honor, and glory to God and to my Lord and Savior, Jesus Christ, for His reassuring, awesome, all-powerful Word, for His blessed promises, and for His loving-kindness and His tender mercies that are new every morning. I am grateful for life.

I pray that as you open this book and look to God for His love, His protection, and His guidance, you will experience His presence and the power of His Holy Spirit; that He will transform and deliver you from whatever situation you are confronted by; and that He will bless, keep, and guide you in His way everlasting.

Jesus said, "Peace I leave with you, my peace I give unto you: not as the world giveth, give I unto you. Let not your heart be troubled; neither let it be afraid" (John 14:27).

Introduction

The scriptures and prayers in this book were written to aid your spiritual growth and walk with the Lord. The best advice I can give is for you to make Jesus the Lord of your life, to study the Word of God and hide God's Word in your heart that you might not sin against Him. And in your quest to hold on to God's unchanging hand, you can pray a simple prayer:

Dear Father God,

I confess to You that I am a sinner (Romans 3:23). I am sorry I have sinned against You. I repent of my sins (Acts 3:19; Matthew 4:17), for I believe that Jesus died for my sins (Romans 10:9) and that God raised Him up with all power in His hands (Matthew 28:18), according to the scriptures (1 Corinthians 15:4). Please come into my heart and save me. Save me, God, and my household and be the Lord of my life. And then, please, God, let Your blessings and favor come upon me; confirm and establish the works of my hand, the words of my mouth, and the meditations of my heart, in Jesus's name. Amen.

If you are in need of a Bible, please do not hesitate to send your request to: Exalt JESUS Ministries, PO Box 848, New York, NY 10030. Or send an email to drzsldinkins@yahoo.com. For continued spiritual guidance, you may visit our website at www.zaziizdinkins.com.

Hold on to God's unchanging hand and pray! God is faithful.

Hold on to God's Unchanging Hand and Pray!

Have not I commanded thee? Be strong and of a good courage; be not afraid, neither be thou dismayed; for the LORD thy God is with thee whithersoever thou goest.

—JOSHUA 1:9

Prayer

Dear Father God, I thank You for Your command. I will be strong and courageous! I will not be afraid or discouraged, for you, O Lord, are my God, and You are with me wherever I go, in Jesus's name. Amen.

Cast thy burden upon the LORD and he shall sustain thee: he shall never suffer the righteous to be moved. (Psalm 55:22)

Prayer

Dear Father God, I give my burdens to You, and I thank You that You will take care of me. I thank You that You will always keep me in paths of your righteousness, in Jesus's name. Amen.

For Your Meditation

Blessed is the man that walketh not in the counsel of the ungodly,
nor standeth in the way of sinners, nor sitteth in the seat of the scornful.
But his delight is in the law of the LORD;
and in his law doth he meditate day and night.
And he shall be like a tree planted by the rivers of water,
that bringeth forth his fruit in his season;
his leaf also shall not wither; and whatsoever he doeth shall prosper.

The ungodly are not so: but are like the chaff which the wind driveth away.

Therefore the ungodly shall not stand in the judgment,

nor sinners in the congregation of the righteous.

For the LORD knoweth the way of the righteous:

but the way of the ungodly shall perish. (Psalm 1:1–6)

Hold on to God's Unchanging Hand and Pray!

And be not conformed to this world: but be ye transformed
by the renewing of your mind, that ye may prove what
is that good, and acceptable, and perfect, will of God.

—ROMANS 12:2

Prayer

Dear Father God, I ask that You please help me not to copy
the behavior and customs of this world, but transform me
into a new person by changing the way I think. Help me,
O God, to learn to know Your will for me, which is good
and pleasing and perfect, in Jesus's name. Amen.

Jesus said unto him, If thou canst believe, all things are possible to him that believeth. (Mark 9:23)

Prayer

Dear Father God, I ask that You please help my unbelief. I thank You that anything is possible if a person believes, in Jesus's name. Amen.

For Your Meditation

O LORD our Lord, how excellent is thy name in all the earth!
who hast set thy glory above the heavens.
Out of the mouth of babes and sucklings hast thou ordained strength
because of thine enemies,
that thou mightest still the enemy and the avenger.
When I consider thy heavens,
the work of thy fingers, the moon and the stars, which thou hast ordained;
What is man, that thou art mindful of him? and the son of man, that thou visitest him?

For thou hast made him a little lower than the angels,

and hast crowned him with glory and honour.

Thou madest him to have dominion over the works of thy hands;

thou hast put all things under his feet:

All sheep and oxen, yea, and the beasts of the field;

The fowl of the air, and the fish of the sea,

and whatsoever passeth through the paths of the seas.

O LORD our Lord, how excellent is thy name in all the earth! (Psalm 8:1–9)

Hold on to God's Unchanging Hand and Pray!

I can do all things through Christ which strengtheneth me.
— PHILIPPIANS 4:13

Prayer

Dear Father God, I thank You that I can do everything through Your Son, Christ Jesus, who gives me strength, in Jesus's name. Amen.

> Blessed is the man that trusteth in the LORD, and whose hope the LORD is. (Jeremiah 17:7)

Prayer

Dear Father God, I thank You for Your many blessings, for I have put my trust in You and have made You my hope and confidence, in Jesus's name. Amen.

> All the paths of the LORD are mercy and truth unto such as keep his covenant and his testimonies. (Psalm 25:10)

Prayer

Dear Father God, I thank You for leading me with Your unfailing love and faithfulness and for helping me to keep Your covenant and to obey Your testimonies, in Jesus's name. Amen.

For Your Meditation

> The heavens declare the glory of God; and the firmament sheweth his handywork.
> Day unto day uttereth speech, and night unto night sheweth knowledge.
> There is no speech nor language, where their voice is not heard.

Their line is gone out through all the earth,
and their words to the end of the world.
In them hath he set a tabernacle for the sun,
Which is as a bridegroom coming out of his chamber,
and rejoiceth as a strong man to run a race.
His going forth is from the end of the heaven,
and his circuit unto the ends of it:
and there is nothing hid from the heat thereof.
The law of the LORD is perfect, converting the soul:
the testimony of the LORD is sure, making wise the simple.
The statutes of the LORD are right, rejoicing the heart:
the commandment of the LORD is pure, enlightening the eyes.
The fear of the LORD is clean, enduring forever:
the judgments of the LORD are true and righteous altogether.
More to be desired are they than gold, yea, than much fine gold:
sweeter also than honey and the honeycomb.

Moreover by them is thy servant warned: and in keeping of them there is great reward.

Who can understand his errors?

Cleanse thou me from secret faults.

Keep back thy servant also from presumptuous sins; let them not have dominion over me:

then shall I be upright, and I shall be innocent from the great transgression.

Let the words of my mouth, and the meditation of my heart, be acceptable in thy sight,

O LORD, my strength, and my redeemer. (Psalm 19:1–14)

Hold on to God's Unchanging Hand and Pray!

Come unto me, all ye that labour and are heavy laden, and I will give you rest.
—MATTHEW 11:28

Prayer

Dear Father God, I thank You that I can come to You with my heavy burdens and that You will give me rest, in Jesus's name. Amen.

> And the LORD, he it is that doth go before thee; he will be with thee, he will not fail thee, neither forsake thee: fear not, neither be dismayed. (Deuteronomy 31:8)

Prayer

Dear Father God, I thank You that I need not be afraid or discouraged, for You will personally go ahead of me. And You will be with me and will neither fail me nor abandon me, in Jesus's name. Amen.

For Your Meditation

The LORD is my shepherd;
I shall not want.
He maketh me to lie down in green pastures:
he leadeth me beside the still waters.
He restoreth my soul:
he leadeth me in the paths of righteousness
for his name's sake.
Yea, though I walk through the valley of the
shadow of death, I will fear no evil:
for thou art with me;
thy rod and thy staff they comfort me.
Thou preparest a table before me in the
presence of mine enemies:
thou anointest my head with oil; my cup
runneth over.

Surely goodness and mercy shall follow me
all the days of my life:
and I will dwell in the house of the LORD
forever. (Psalm 23:1–6)

Hold on to God's Unchanging Hand and Pray!

Let your conversation be without covetousness; and be content with such things as ye have: for he hath said, I will never leave thee, nor forsake thee.

—HEBREWS 13:5

Prayer

Dear Father God, I ask that You please help me to be satisfied with what You have given to me. I thank You that You will never leave me or forsake me, in Jesus's name. Amen.

> Pleasant words are as an honeycomb, sweet to the soul, and health to the bones. (Proverbs 16:24)

Prayer

Dear Father God, I ask that You please help me to speak only kind words that are like honey—sweet to the soul and healthy for the body, in Jesus's name. Amen.

For Your Meditation

The earth is the LORD'S, and the fulness thereof; the world, and they that dwell therein.

For he hath founded it upon the seas, and established it upon the floods.

Who shall ascend into the hill of the LORD? or who shall stand in his holy place?

He that hath clean hands, and a pure heart; who hath not lifted up his soul unto vanity, nor sworn deceitfully.

He shall receive the blessing from the LORD, and righteousness from the God of his salvation.

This is the generation of them that seek him, that seek thy face, O Jacob. Selah.

Lift up your heads, O ye gates; and be ye lift up, ye everlasting doors;

and the King of glory shall come in.

Who is this King of glory?

The LORD strong and mighty, the LORD mighty in battle.

Lift up your heads, O ye gates; even lift them up, ye everlasting doors; and the King of glory shall come in.

Who is this King of glory?

The LORD of hosts, he is the King of glory.

Selah. (Psalm 24:1–10)

Hold on to God's Unchanging Hand and Pray!

This is the day which the LORD hath made;
we will rejoice and be glad in it.

—PSALM 118:24

Prayer

Dear Father God, I thank You for this day that You have made. I will rejoice and be glad. I will enjoy it, in Jesus's name. Amen.

> But as it is written Eye hath not seen, nor ear heard, neither have entered into the heart of man, the things which God hath prepared for them that love him. But God

hath revealed them unto us by his Spirit: for the Spirit searcheth all things, yea the deep things of God. (1 Corinthians 2:9–10)

Prayer

Dear Father God, I thank You that no eye has seen, no ear has heard, and no mind has ever imagined the things You have prepared for me and others who love You. I thank You that, even so, You have revealed them by Your Holy Spirit, for Your Spirit searches all things that are of You, O God. Thank You, in Jesus's name. Amen.

For Your Meditation

The LORD is my light and my salvation; whom shall I fear?
the LORD is the strength of my life; of whom shall I be afraid?
When the wicked, even mine enemies and my foes, came upon me to eat up my flesh, they stumbled and fell.
Though an host should encamp against me, my heart shall not fear:

though war should rise against me, in this will I be confident.

One thing have I desired of the LORD, that will I seek after;

that I may dwell in the house of the LORD all the days of my life,

to behold the beauty of the LORD, and to enquire in his temple.

For in the time of trouble he shall hide me in his pavilion:

in the secret of his tabernacle shall he hide me;

he shall set me up upon a rock.

And now shall mine head be lifted up above mine enemies round about me:

therefore will I offer in his tabernacle sacrifices of joy;

I will sing, yea, I will sing praises unto the LORD.

Hear, O LORD, when I cry with my voice: have mercy also upon me, and answer me.

When thou saidst, Seek ye my face; my heart said unto thee,

Thy face, LORD, will I seek.

Hide not thy face far from me; put not thy servant away in anger:

thou hast been my help; leave me not, neither forsake me,

O God of my salvation.

When my father and my mother forsake me, then the LORD will take me up.

Teach me thy way, O LORD, and lead me in a plain path, because of mine enemies.

Deliver me not over unto the will of mine enemies:

for false witnesses are risen up against me, and such as breathe out cruelty.

I had fainted, unless I had believed to see the goodness of the LORD

in the land of the living.

Wait on the LORD: be of good courage, and he shall strengthen thine heart:

wait, I say, on the LORD. (Psalm 27:1–14)

Hold on to God's Unchanging Hand and Pray!

Who shall separate us from the love of Christ? shall tribulation, or distress, or persecution, or famine, or nakedness, or peril, or sword? As it is written, For thy sake we are killed all the day long; we are accounted as sheep for the slaughter. Nay, in all these things we are more than conquerors through him that loved us. For I am persuaded, that neither death, nor life, nor angels, nor principalities, nor powers, nor things present, nor things to come, Nor height, nor depth, nor any other creature, shall be able to separate us from the love of God, which is in Christ Jesus our Lord.

—ROMANS 8:35–39

Prayer

Dear God, I thank You that there isn't anything that can ever separate me from the love of Christ. I thank You that it does not mean that He no longer loves me if I have trouble or calamity, or if I'm persecuted, or hungry, or destitute, or in danger, or threatened with death. For as the scriptures say, for Your sake, I am killed every day; I am being slaughtered like a sheep. So, despite all these things, I am grateful and thankful that overwhelming victory is mine through Christ who loves me. And I am convinced that nothing can ever separate me from Your love. Neither death nor life, neither angels nor demons, neither my fears for today nor my worries about tomorrow—not even the powers of hell can separate me from Your love. No power in the sky above or in the earth below—indeed, nothing in all creation will ever be able to separate me from Your love that is revealed in Christ Jesus, my Lord. Thank You, God, in Jesus's name. Amen.

For Your Meditation

I will exalt you, LORD, for you rescued me. You refused to let my enemies triumph over me.

O LORD my God, I cried to you for help, and you restored my health.

You brought me up from the grave, O LORD. You kept me from falling into the pit of death.... You have turned my mourning into joyful dancing.

You have taken away my clothes of mourning and clothed me with joy;

that I might sing praises to you and not be silent.

O LORD my God, I will give you thanks forever! (Psalm 30:1–3, 11–12)

Hold on to God's Unchanging Hand and Pray!

My flesh and my heart faileth: but God is the strength of my heart, and my portion forever.

—PSALM 73:26

Prayer

Dear Father God, I thank You that even if my health fails and my spirit grows weak, You, O God, remain the strength of my heart, and You are mine forever, in Jesus's name. Amen.

But they that wait upon the LORD shall renew their strength; they shall mount up with wings as eagles; they shall run, and not

be weary; and they shall walk, and not faint.
(Isaiah 40:31)

Prayer

Dear Father God, I thank You for giving me new strength
as I put my trust in You. I thank You for making me to
soar high on wings like eagles; for helping me to run and
not grow weary; and for helping me to walk and not faint,
in Jesus's name. Amen.

For Your Meditation

I will bless the LORD at all times: his praise
shall continually be in my mouth.
My soul shall make her boast in the LORD:
the humble shall hear thereof, and be glad.
O magnify the LORD with me, and let us
exalt his name together.
I sought the LORD, and he heard me, and
delivered me from all my fears.
They looked unto him, and were lightened:
and their faces were not ashamed.
This poor man cried, and the LORD heard
him, and saved him out of all his troubles.

The angel of the LORD encampeth round about them that fear him, and delivereth them.

O taste and see that the LORD is good: blessed is the man that trusteth in him.

O fear the LORD, ye his saints: for there is no want to them that fear him.

The young lions do lack, and suffer hunger: but they that seek the LORD shall not want any good thing.

Come, ye children, hearken unto me: I will teach you the fear of the LORD.

What man is he that desireth life, and loveth many days, that he may see good?

Keep thy tongue from evil, and thy lips from speaking guile.

Depart from evil, and do good; seek peace, and pursue it.

The eyes of the LORD are upon the righteous, and his ears are open unto their cry.

The face of the LORD is against them that do evil,

to cut off the remembrance of them from the earth.

The righteous cry, and the LORD heareth, and delivereth them out of all their troubles.

The LORD is nigh unto them that are of a broken heart;

and saveth such as be of a contrite spirit.

Many are the afflictions of the righteous:

but the LORD delivereth him out of them all.

He keepeth all his bones: not one of them is broken.

Evil shall slay the wicked: and they that hate the righteous shall be desolate.

The LORD redeemeth the soul of his servants:

and none of them that trust in him shall be desolate. (Psalm 34:1–22)

Hold on to God's Unchanging Hand and Pray!

Behold, what manner of love the Father hath bestowed upon us, that we should be called the sons of God: therefore the world knoweth us not, because it knew him not.

—1 John 3:1

Prayer

Dear Father God, I thank You for how much You love me and how You refer to me as Your child, for that's what I am. I pray for those in the world who do not recognize Your children because they don't know You. I pray that they too will one day come to know You, that they may become Your children also, in Jesus's name. Amen.

But he said, Yea rather, blessed are they that hear the word of God, and keep it. (Luke 11:28)

Prayer

Dear Father God, I thank You for Your many blessings and that You have enabled me to hear Your Word. I pray that You will continue to help me to keep Your Word and put it into practice, in Jesus's name. Amen.

For Your Meditation

Fret not thyself because of evildoers, neither be thou envious against the workers of iniquity.
For they shall soon be cut down like the grass, and wither as the green herb.
Trust in the LORD, and do good; so shalt thou dwell in the land, and verily thou shalt be fed.
Delight thyself also in the LORD; and he shall give thee the desires of thine heart.
Commit thy way unto the LORD; trust also in him; and he shall bring it to pass.

And he shall bring forth thy righteousness as the light, and thy judgment as the noonday.

Rest in the LORD, and wait patiently for him: fret not thyself because of him who prospereth in his way,

because of the man who bringeth wicked devices to pass.

Cease from anger, and forsake wrath: fret not thyself in any wise to do evil.

For evildoers shall be cut off: but those that wait upon the LORD, they shall inherit the earth.

For yet a little while, and the wicked shall not be: yea, thou shalt diligently consider his place, and it shall not be.

But the meek shall inherit the earth; and shall delight themselves in the abundance of peace.

The wicked plotteth against the just, and gnasheth upon him with his teeth.

The Lord shall laugh at him: for he seeth that his day is coming.

The wicked have drawn out the sword, and have bent their bow, to cast down the poor and needy,

and to slay such as be of upright conversation.
Their sword shall enter into their own heart,
and their bows shall be broken.
A little that a righteous man hath is better
than the riches of many wicked.
For the arms of the wicked shall be broken:
but the LORD upholdeth the righteous.
The LORD knoweth the days of the upright:
and their inheritance shall be forever.
They shall not be ashamed in the evil time:
and in the days of famine they shall be
satisfied.
But the wicked shall perish,
and the enemies of the LORD shall be as the
fat of lambs:
they shall consume; into smoke shall they
consume away.
The wicked borroweth, and payeth not
again:
but the righteous sheweth mercy, and giveth.
For such as be blessed of him shall inherit
the earth;
and they that be cursed of him shall be
cut off.
The steps of a good man are ordered by the
LORD: and he delighteth in his way.

Though he fall, he shall not be utterly cast down:

for the LORD upholdeth him with his hand.

I have been young, and now am old;

yet have I not seen the righteous forsaken, nor his seed begging bread.

He is ever merciful, and lendeth; and his seed is blessed.

Depart from evil, and do good; and dwell for evermore.

For the LORD loveth judgment, and forsaketh not his saints;

they are preserved for ever: but the seed of the wicked shall be cut off.

The righteous shall inherit the land, and dwell therein forever.

The mouth of the righteous speaketh wisdom, and his tongue talketh of judgment.

The law of his God is in his heart; none of his steps shall slide.

The wicked watcheth the righteous, and seeketh to slay him.

The LORD will not leave him in his hand, nor condemn him when he is judged.

Wait on the LORD, and keep his way, and he shall exalt thee to inherit the land:

when the wicked are cut off, thou shalt see it.

I have seen the wicked in great power, and spreading himself like a green bay tree.

Yet he passed away, and, lo, he was not:

yea, I sought him, but he could not be found. Mark the perfect man, and behold the upright: for the end of that man is peace.

But the transgressors shall be destroyed together:

the end of the wicked shall be cut off.

But the salvation of the righteous is of the LORD:

he is their strength in the time of trouble.

And the LORD shall help them, and deliver them:

he shall deliver them from the wicked, and save them, because they trust in him.

(Psalm 37:1–40)

Hold on to God's Unchanging Hand and Pray!

Thou stretchedst out thy right hand,
the earth swallowed them.

—EXODUS 15:12

Prayer

Dear Father God, I thank You that You raised Your right hand, and the earth swallowed our enemies. Thank You, in Jesus's name. Amen.

Now the Lord of peace himself give you peace always by all means. The Lord be with you all. (2 Thessalonians 3:16)

Prayer

Dear Father God, I thank You for giving me Your peace at all times and in every situation, and I thank You for never leaving me or forsaking me, in Jesus's name. Amen.

> And let the peace of God rule in your hearts,
> to the which also ye are called in one body;
> and be ye thankful. (Colossians 3:15)

Prayer

Dear Father God, I thank You that the peace that comes from You rules my heart. Help me to continue to live in peace and always be grateful, in Jesus's name. Amen.

For Your Meditation

> God is our refuge and strength, a very present help in trouble.
> Therefore will not we fear,
> though the earth be removed, and though the mountains be carried into the midst of the sea;
> Though the waters thereof roar and be troubled,

though the mountains shake with the swelling thereof. Selah.

There is a river, the streams whereof shall make glad the city of God,

the holy place of the tabernacles of the most High.

God is in the midst of her;

she shall not be moved: God shall help her, and that right early.

The heathen raged, the kingdoms were moved: he uttered his voice, the earth melted.

The LORD of hosts is with us;

the God of Jacob is our refuge. Selah.

Come, behold the works of the LORD, what desolations he hath made in the earth.

He maketh wars to cease unto the end of the earth;

he breaketh the bow, and cutteth the spear in sunder;

he burneth the chariot in the fire.

Be still, and know that I am God:

I will be exalted among the heathen, I will be exalted in the earth.

The LORD of hosts is with us; the God of Jacob is our refuge. Selah. (Psalm 46:1–11)

Hold on to God's Unchanging Hand and Pray!

O LORD my God, I cried unto thee,
and thou hast healed me.

—Psalm 30:2

Prayer

Dear Father God, I thank You, and I am so grateful, for I cried to You for help, and You restored my health. Thank You, in Jesus's name. Amen.

> And whosoever shall exalt himself shall be abased; and he that shall humble himself shall be exalted. (Matthew 23:12)

Prayer

Dear Father God, I ask that You please help me to stay humble and not to exalt myself, for it's in You that I move and have my being, and my works are unto You. Whatever I do, dear God, I do all to Your glory, in Jesus's name. Amen.

> But now thus saith the LORD that created thee, O Jacob, and he that formed thee, O Israel, Fear not: for I have redeemed thee, I have called thee by thy name; thou art mine. When thou passest through the waters, I will be with thee; and through the rivers, they shall not overflow thee: when thou walkest through the fire, thou shalt not be burned; neither shall the flame kindle upon thee. (Isaiah 43:1–2)

Prayer

Dear Father God, please help me to listen to You who created me—for You who have formed me, have said that I should not be afraid, have ransomed me. You have called me by name; I am Yours. When I go through deep waters, You will be with me. When I go through the rivers of difficulty, I will not drown. When I walk through the fire of oppression, I will not be burned up; the flames will not consume me. Thank You, God, in Jesus's name. Amen.

For Your Meditation

Have mercy upon me, O God, according to thy lovingkindness:
according unto the multitude of thy tender mercies blot out my transgressions.
Wash me throughly from mine iniquity, and cleanse me from my sin.
For I acknowledge my transgressions: and my sin is ever before me.
Against thee, thee only, have I sinned, and done this evil in thy sight:
that thou mightest be justified when thou speakest, and be clear when thou judgest.
Behold, I was shapen in iniquity; and in sin did my mother conceive me.
Behold, thou desirest truth in the inward parts: and in the hidden part thou shalt make me to know wisdom. Purge me with hyssop, and I shall be clean:
wash me, and I shall be whiter than snow.

Make me to hear joy and gladness; that the bones which thou hast broken may rejoice.

Hide thy face from my sins, and blot out all mine iniquities.

Create in me a clean heart, O God; and renew a right spirit within me.

Cast me not away from thy presence; and take not thy holy spirit from me.

Restore unto me the joy of thy salvation; and uphold me with thy free spirit.

Then will I teach transgressors thy ways; and sinners shall be converted unto thee.

Deliver me from bloodguiltiness, O God, thou God of my salvation:

and my tongue shall sing aloud of thy righteousness.

O Lord, open thou my lips; and my mouth shall shew forth thy praise.

For thou desirest not sacrifice; else would I give it: thou delightest not in burnt offering.

The sacrifices of God are a broken spirit: a broken and a contrite heart, O God, thou wilt not despise.

Do good in thy good pleasure unto Zion: build thou the walls of Jerusalem.

Then shalt thou be pleased with the sacrifices of righteousness,
with burnt offering and whole burnt offering:
then shall they offer bullocks upon thine altar. (Psalm 51:1–19)

Hold on to God's Unchanging Hand and Pray!

And God spake all these words, saying, I am the LORD thy God, which have brought thee out of the land of Egypt, out of the house of bondage. Thou shalt have no other gods before me. Thou shalt not make unto thee any graven image, or any likeness of anything that is in heaven above, or that is in the earth beneath, or that is in the water under the earth: Thou shalt not bow down thyself to them, nor serve them: for I the LORD thy God am a jealous God, visiting the iniquity of the fathers upon the children unto the third and fourth generation of them that hate me; And shewing mercy unto thousands of them that love me, and keep my commandments. Thou shalt not take the name of the LORD thy God in vain; for the LORD will not hold him guiltless that taketh his name in vain. Remember the sabbath day, to keep it holy. Six days shalt thou labour, and do all thy work: But the seventh day is the sabbath of the LORD thy God: in it thou shalt not do any work, thou, nor thy son, nor thy daughter, thy manservant, nor thy maidservant, nor thy cattle, nor thy stranger that is within thy gates: For in six days the LORD made heaven and earth, the sea, and all that in them is, and rested the seventh day: wherefore the LORD blessed the sabbath day, and hallowed it. Honour thy father and thy mother: that thy days may be long upon the land which the LORD thy God giveth thee. Thou shalt not kill. Thou shalt not commit adultery. Thou shalt not steal. Thou shalt not bear false witness against thy neighbour. Thou shalt not covet thy neighbour's house, thou shalt not covet thy neighbour's wife, nor his manservant, nor his maidservant, nor his ox, nor his ass, nor any thing that is thy neighbour's. (Exodus 20:1–17)

Prayer

Dear Father God, I thank You for these instructions that You have given to us, Your people. I receive them with love. For You are the Lord my God, who rescued me from the land of Egypt, the place of my slavery. Please help me to not have any other god but You. Help me to not make for myself an idol of any kind or an image of anything in the heavens or on the earth or in the sea. Help me to not bow down to them or worship them, for You, the Lord my God, are a jealous God who will not tolerate my affection for any other gods. You have laid the sins of the parents upon their children; the entire family is affected—even children in the third and fourth generations of those who reject You. But You lavish Your unfailing love for a thousand generations on those who love You and obey Your commands. Please help me to not misuse Your name, the name of the Lord my God, for I know that You will not let me go unpunished if I misuse Your name. Please help me to remember to observe the Sabbath day by keeping it holy. For I have six days each week for my ordinary work, but the seventh day is a Sabbath day of rest, dedicated to You, the Lord my God. On that day, I pray that no one in my household do any work. This includes myself, my sons and daughters, my male and female servants, and any foreigners living among my family. For in six days, You made the heavens, the earth, the sea, and everything in them; but on the seventh day, You rested. That is why You blessed the Sabbath day and set it apart as holy. Help me to honor my father and mother. Then I will live a long, full life in the land You, O God, are giving me. Be my help always, for I will not murder; I will not commit adultery; I will not steal; I will not testify falsely against my neighbor; I will not covet my neighbor's house; I will not covet my neighbor's wife, male or female servant, ox or donkey, or anything else that belongs to my neighbor, in Jesus's name. Amen.

For Your Meditation

Be merciful unto me, O God, be merciful unto me: for my soul trusteth in thee: yea, in the shadow of thy wings will I make my refuge, until these calamities be overpast.
I will cry unto God most high; unto God that performeth all things for me.
He shall send from heaven, and save me from the reproach of him that would swallow me up. Selah.
God shall send forth his mercy and his truth.

My soul is among lions: and I lie even among them that are set on fire,

even the sons of men, whose teeth are spears and arrows, and their tongue a sharp sword.

Be thou exalted, O God, above the heavens; let thy glory be above all the earth.

They have prepared a net for my steps; my soul is bowed down:

they have digged a pit before me, into the midst whereof they are fallen themselves. Selah.

My heart is fixed, O God, my heart is fixed: I will sing and give praise.

Awake up, my glory; awake, psaltery and harp: I myself will awake early.

I will praise thee, O Lord, among the people: I will sing unto thee among the nations.

For thy mercy is great unto the heavens, and thy truth unto the clouds.

Be thou exalted, O God, above the heavens: let thy glory be above all the earth. (Psalm 57:1–11)

Hold on to God's Unchanging Hand and Pray!

Be still, and know that I am God: I will be exalted among the heathen, I will be exalted in the earth.

—PSALM 46:10

Prayer

Dear Father God, I thank You that I can be still because I know You. I thank You that I belong to You and that You knew me before I was formed in my mother's womb. You will be honored by every nation. You will be honored throughout the world, in Jesus's name. Amen.

> For I know the thoughts that I think toward you, saith the LORD, thoughts of peace,

and not of evil, to give you an expected end.
(Jeremiah 29:11)

Prayer

Dear Father God, I thank You for the plans You have for me. They are plans for good and not for disaster, to give me a future and a hope. Thank You, in Jesus's name. Amen.

> It is better to trust in the LORD than to put confidence in man. (Psalm 118:8)

Prayer

Dear Father God, I thank You that I can take refuge in You, rather than to trust in humankind. Thank You, in Jesus's name. Amen.

For Your Meditation

> Hear my cry, O God; attend unto my prayer. From the end of the earth will I cry unto thee,
> When my heart is overwhelmed: lead me to the rock that is higher than I.

For thou hast been a shelter for me, and a strong tower from the enemy.

I will abide in thy tabernacle for ever.

I will trust in the covert of thy wings. Selah.

For thou, O God, hast heard my vows:

thou has given me the heritage of those that fear thy name.

Thou wilt prolong the king's life: and his years as many generations.

He shall abide before God forever.

O prepare mercy and truth, which may preserve him.

So will I sing praise unto thy name for ever, that I may daily perform my vows. (Psalm 61:1–8)

Hold on to God's Unchanging Hand and Pray!

Behold, I am the LORD, the God of all flesh:
is there anything too hard for me?
—JEREMIAH 32:27

Prayer

Dear Father God, I thank You that You are the Lord, the God of all the people of the world. I thank You, and I am grateful that there is nothing too hard for You, in Jesus's name. Amen.

Fear thou not; for I am with thee: be not dismayed; for I am thy God: I will strengthen thee; yea, I will help thee; yea, I will uphold thee with the right hand of my righteousness. (Isaiah 41:10)

Prayer

Dear Father God, I thank You that I do not need to be afraid, for You are with me. I thank You that I do not need to be discouraged, for You are my God. You will strengthen me and help me. You will hold me up with Your victorious right hand. Thank You, in Jesus's name. Amen.

> For I know that my redeemer liveth, and that he shall stand at the latter day upon the earth: And though after my skin worms destroy this body, yet in my flesh shall I see God: (Job 19:25–26)

Prayer

Dear Father God, thank You for giving me knowledge of You, my Redeemer, who lives and who will stand upon the earth at last. And after my body has decayed, yet in my body I will see You! Thank You, in Jesus's name. Amen.

For Your Meditation

Lord, thou hast been our dwelling place in all generations.

Before the mountains were brought forth, or ever thou hadst formed the earth and the world,

even from everlasting to everlasting, thou art God.

Thou turnest man to destruction; and sayest, Return, ye children of men.

For a thousand years in thy sight are but as yesterday when it is past, and as a watch in the night.

Thou carriest them away as with a flood; they are as a sleep:

in the morning they are like grass which groweth up.

In the morning it flourisheth, and groweth up; in the evening it is cut down, and withereth.

For we are consumed by thine anger, and by thy wrath are we troubled.

Thou hast set our iniquities before thee, our secret sins in the light of thy countenance.

For all our days are passed away in thy wrath:

we spend our years as a tale that is told.

The days of our years are threescore years and ten;

and if by reason of strength they be fourscore years,

yet is their strength labour and sorrow; for it is soon cut off, and we fly away.

Who knoweth the power of thine anger? even according to thy fear, so is thy wrath.

So teach us to number our days, that we may apply our hearts unto wisdom.

Return, O LORD, how long? and let it repent thee concerning thy servants.

O satisfy us early with thy mercy; that we may rejoice and be glad all our days.

Make us glad according to the days wherein thou hast afflicted us,

and the years wherein we have seen evil.

Let thy work appear unto thy servants, and thy glory unto their children.

And let the beauty of the LORD our God be upon us:

and establish thou the work of our hands upon us;

yea, the work of our hands establish thou it. (Psalm 90:1–17)

Hold on to God's Unchanging Hand and Pray!

No weapon that is formed against thee shall prosper; and every tongue that shall rise against thee in judgment thou shalt condemn. This is the heritage of the servants of the LORD, and their righteousness is of me, saith the LORD.

—Isaiah 54:17

Prayer

Dear Father God, I thank You that in that coming day, no weapon turned against me will succeed. You will silence every voice raised up to accuse me. Thank You for these benefits I enjoy as Your servant, for my vindication will come from You, just as You have spoken! Thank You, in Jesus's name. Amen.

Dr. Z. S. L. Dinkins, ThD, DBA

For though we walk in the flesh, we do not war after the flesh: (For the weapons of our warfare are not carnal, but mighty through God to the pulling down of strong holds). (2 Corinthians 10:3–4)

Prayer

Dear Father God, I thank You that we Christians are human, but we don't wage war as humans do. We use Your mighty spiritual weapons, not worldly weapons, to knock down the strongholds of human reasoning and to destroy false arguments, in Jesus's name. Amen.

For Your Meditation

He that dwelleth in the secret place of the most High
shall abide under the shadow of the Almighty.
I will say of the LORD, He is my refuge and my fortress: my God; in him will I trust.
Surely he shall deliver thee from the snare of the fowler, and from the noisome pestilence.

He shall cover thee with his feathers, and under his wings shalt thou trust:
his truth shall be thy shield and buckler.
Thou shalt not be afraid for the terror by night; nor for the arrow that flieth by day;
Nor for the pestilence that walketh in darkness; nor for the destruction that wasteth at noonday.
A thousand shall fall at thy side, and ten thousand at thy right hand;
but it shall not come nigh thee.
Only with thine eyes shalt thou behold and see the reward of the wicked.
Because thou hast made the LORD, which is my refuge, even the most High, thy habitation;
There shall no evil befall thee, neither shall any plague come nigh thy dwelling.
For he shall give his angels charge over thee, to keep thee in all thy ways.
They shall bear thee up in their hands, lest thou dash thy foot against a stone.
Thou shalt tread upon the lion and adder: the young lion and the dragon shalt thou trample under feet.

Because he hath set his love upon me, therefore will I deliver him:
I will set him on high, because he hath known my name.
He shall call upon me, and I will answer him: I will be with him in trouble;
I will deliver him, and honour him.
With long life will I satisfy him, and shew him my salvation. (Psalm 91:1–16)

Hold on to God's Unchanging Hand and Pray!

If ye abide in me, and my words abide in you, ye shall ask what ye will, and it shall be done unto you.

—JOHN 15:7

Prayer

Dear Father God, I thank You that if I remain in You and Your words remain in me, I may ask for anything that is of Your will and it shall be granted, in Jesus's name. Amen.

Rejoice in the Lord alway: and again I say, Rejoice. (Philippians 4:4)

DR. Z. S. L. DINKINS, ThD, DBA

Prayer

Dear Father God, I ask that You please always fill me with Your joy, that I may rejoice in You again and again, in Jesus's name. Amen.

> And he said unto me, My grace is sufficient for thee: for my strength is made perfect in weakness. Most gladly therefore will I rather glory in my infirmities, that the power of Christ may rest upon me. (2 Corinthians 12:9)

Prayer

Dear Father God, I thank You for each time You said, "My grace is all You need. My power works best in weakness." So now I am glad to boast about my weaknesses, so that the power of Christ can work through me. Thank You, in Jesus's name. Amen.

For Your Meditation

> Make a joyful noise unto the LORD, all ye lands.
> Serve the LORD with gladness:

come before his presence with singing.

Know ye that the LORD he is God: it is he that hath made us, and not we ourselves; we are his people, and the sheep of his pasture.

Enter into his gates with thanksgiving, and into his courts with praise: be thankful unto him, and bless his name.

For the LORD is good; his mercy is everlasting; and his truth endureth to all generations. (Psalm 100:1–5)

Hold on to God's Unchanging Hand and Pray!

But seek ye first the kingdom of God, and his righteousness; and all these things shall be added unto you.

— MATTHEW 6:33

Prayer

Dear Father God, I thank You that if I seek Your kingdom above all else and live righteously, You will give me everything I need. Thank You, in Jesus's name. Amen.

Ask, and it shall be given you; seek, and ye shall find; knock, and it shall be opened unto you: For every one that asketh receiveth;

and he that seeketh findeth; and to him that knocketh it shall be opened. (Matthew 7:7–8)

Prayer

Dear Father God, I thank You for Your encouragement. I thank You that, if I keep on asking, I will receive what I ask for; if I keep on seeking, I will find what I am looking for; and if I keep on knocking, the door will eventually be opened to me. For as Your word has declared, everyone who asks receives; everyone who seeks finds; and to everyone who knocks, the door opens. Thank You, in Jesus's name. Amen.

Hear, O Israel: The LORD our God is one LORD: And thou shalt love the LORD thy God with all thine heart, and with all thy soul, and with all thy might. (Deuteronomy 6:4–5)

Prayer

Dear Father God, I praise You that You, the LORD my God, are LORD alone. I love You with all my heart, and with all my soul, and with all my strength, in Jesus's name. Amen.

For Your Meditation

Bless the LORD, O my soul: and all that is within me, bless his holy name.

Bless the LORD, O my soul, and forget not all his benefits:

Who forgiveth all thine iniquities; who healeth all thy diseases;

Who redeemeth thy life from destruction; who crowneth thee with lovingkindness and tender mercies;

Who satisfieth thy mouth with good things; so that thy youth is renewed like the eagle's.

The LORD executeth righteousness and judgment for all that are oppressed.

He made known his ways unto Moses, his acts unto the children of Israel.

The LORD is merciful and gracious, slow to anger, and plenteous in mercy.

He will not always chide: neither will he keep his anger for ever.

He hath not dealt with us after our sins; nor rewarded us according to our iniquities.

For as the heaven is high above the earth, so great is his mercy toward them that fear him.

As far as the east is from the west, so
far hath he removed our transgressions
from us.

Like as a father pitieth his children, so the
LORD pitieth them that fear him.

For he knoweth our frame; he remembereth
that we are dust.

As for man, his days are as grass: as a flower
of the field, so he flourisheth.

For the wind passeth over it, and it is gone;
and the place thereof shall know it no more.

But the mercy of the LORD is from
everlasting to everlasting upon them that
fear him,

and his righteousness unto children's
children;

To such as keep his covenant, and to those
that remember his commandments to do
them.

The LORD hath prepared his throne in the
heavens; and his kingdom ruleth over all.

Bless the LORD, ye his angels, that excel in
strength,

that do his commandments, hearkening
unto the voice of his word.

Bless ye the LORD, all ye his hosts; ye ministers of his, that do his pleasure.

Bless the LORD, all his works in all places of his dominion: bless the LORD, O my soul. (Psalm 103:1–22)

Hold on to God's Unchanging Hand and Pray!

*Jesus said unto him, Thou shalt love the Lord
thy God with all thy heart, and with all thy soul,
and with all thy mind. This is the first and great
commandment. And the second is like unto it, Thou
shalt love thy neighbour as thyself. On these two
commandments hang all the law and the prophets.*

—MATTHEW 22:37-40

Prayer

Dear Father God, I thank You for teaching us what is
important in life, that we must love You, the Lord our
God, with all our heart, all our soul, and all our mind,
for this is the first and greatest commandment. And

the second is equally important: that we must love our neighbor as ourselves. Thank You that the entire law and all the demands of the prophets are based on these two commandments, in Jesus's name. Amen.

Pray without ceasing. (1 Thessalonians 5:17)

Prayer

Dear Father God, I thank You for hearing my prayers. Help me to continuously pray that my requests may be made known unto You, O God, in Jesus's name. Amen.

> But I would not have you to be ignorant, brethren, concerning them which are asleep, that ye sorrow not, even as others which have no hope. For if we believe that Jesus died and rose again, even so them also which sleep in Jesus will God bring with him. For this we say unto you by the word of the Lord, that we which are alive and remain unto the coming of the Lord shall not prevent them which are asleep. For the Lord himself shall descend from heaven with a shout, with the voice of the archangel, and with the trump of God: and the dead in Christ shall rise

first: Then we which are alive and remain shall be caught up together with them in the clouds, to meet the Lord in the air: and so shall we ever be with the Lord. Wherefore comfort one another with these words. (1 Thessalonians 4:13–18)

Prayer

Dear Father God, I thank You for letting us know what will happen to the believers who have died so we do not grieve like people who have no hope. For since we believe that Jesus died and was raised to life again, we also believe that when Jesus returns, You will bring back with Him the believers who have died. Thank You for telling us that directly: we who are still living when Jesus returns will not meet Him ahead of those who have died. For Jesus Himself will come down from heaven with a commanding shout, with the voice of the archangel, and with Your trumpet call. Then, first, the believers who have died will rise from their graves, and together with them, we who are still alive and remain on the earth will be caught up in the clouds to meet Jesus in the air. Then we will be with Jesus forever. Help us to encourage one another with these words, in Jesus's name. Amen.

For Your Meditation

O praise the LORD, all ye nations: praise him, all ye people.

For his merciful kindness is great toward us: and the truth of the LORD endureth for ever.

Praise ye the LORD. (Psalm 117:1–2)

Hold on to God's Unchanging Hand and Pray!

Jesus said unto her, I am the resurrection, and the life: he that believeth in me, though he were dead, yet shall he live: And whosoever liveth and believeth in me shall never die. Believest thou this?

—John 11:25–26

Prayer

Dear Father God, I thank You that Your Son, Jesus, is the resurrection and the life, and anyone who believes in Jesus will live, even after dying. Thank You that everyone who lives in Jesus and believes in Jesus will never ever die. I believe this, Lord. Thank You, in Jesus's name. Amen.

In my Father's house are many mansions:
if it were not so, I would have told you. I go
to prepare a place for you. And if I go and
prepare a place for you, I will come again,
and receive you unto myself; that where I
am, there ye may be also. (John 14:2–3)

Prayer

Dear Father God, I thank You that there is more than
enough room in Your home. Thank You for preparing
a place for me. And thank You that when everything is
ready, You will come and get me, so that I will always
be with You where You are. Thank You, in Jesus's name.
Amen.

Jesus saith unto him, I am the way, the truth,
and the life: no man cometh unto the Father,
but by me. (John 14:6)

Prayer

Dear Father God, I thank You for Your Son, Jesus. Thank
You that Jesus is the way, the truth, and the life. Thank You
that no one can come to You, the Father, except through
Jesus. Thank You, in Jesus's name. Amen.

For Your Meditation

I will lift up mine eyes unto the hills, from whence cometh my help.

My help cometh from the LORD, which made heaven and earth.

He will not suffer thy foot to be moved: he that keepeth thee will not slumber.

Behold, he that keepeth Israel shall neither slumber nor sleep.

The LORD is thy keeper: the LORD is thy shade upon thy right hand.

The sun shall not smite thee by day, nor the moon by night.

The LORD shall preserve thee from all evil: he shall preserve thy soul.

The LORD shall preserve thy going out and thy coming in

from this time forth, and even for evermore. (Psalm 121:1–8)

Hold on to God's Unchanging Hand and Pray!

And ye shall know the truth, and the
truth shall make you free.
—JOHN 8:32

Prayer

Dear Father God, I praise and thank You for giving me knowledge of the truth and that the truth has set me free. Thank You, in Jesus's name. Amen.

> Thy word is a lamp unto my feet, and a light unto my path. (Psalm 119:105)

Prayer

Dear Father God, I thank You for Your Word. Your Word is a lamp to guide my feet and a light for my path. Thank You, in Jesus's name. Amen.

> Trust in the LORD, and do good; so shalt thou dwell in the land, and verily thou shalt be fed. (Psalm 37:3)

Prayer

Dear Father God, I will always put my trust in You and do good. Thank You for helping me to live safely in the land and to prosper. Thank You, in Jesus's name. Amen.

For Your Meditation

> O LORD, thou hast searched me, and known me.
> Thou knowest my downsitting and mine uprising, thou understandest my thought afar off.
> Thou compassest my path and my lying down, and art acquainted with all my ways.

For there is not a word in my tongue, but, lo, O LORD, thou knowest it altogether.

Thou hast beset me behind and before, and laid thine hand upon me.

Such knowledge is too wonderful for me; it is high, I cannot attain unto it.

Whither shall I go from thy spirit? or whither shall I flee from thy presence?

If I ascend up into heaven, thou art there: if I make my bed in hell, behold, thou art there.

If I take the wings of the morning, and dwell in the uttermost parts of the sea;

Even there shall thy hand lead me, and thy right hand shall hold me.

If I say, Surely the darkness shall cover me; even the night shall be light about me.

Yea, the darkness hideth not from thee; but the night shineth as the day:

the darkness and the light are both alike to thee.

For thou hast possessed my reins: thou hast covered me in my mother's womb.

I will praise thee; for I am fearfully and wonderfully made:

marvellous are thy works; and that my soul knoweth right well.

My substance was not hid from thee, when
I was made in secret,

and curiously wrought in the lowest parts
of the earth.

Thine eyes did see my substance, yet being
unperfect;

and in thy book all my members were
written,

which in continuance were fashioned, when
as yet there was none of them.

How precious also are thy thoughts unto me,
O God!

how great is the sum of them!

If I should count them, they are more in
number than the sand:

when I awake, I am still with thee.

Surely thou wilt slay the wicked, O God:

depart from me therefore, ye bloody men.

For they speak against thee wickedly, and
thine enemies take thy name in vain.

Do not I hate them, O LORD, that hate thee?

and am not I grieved with those that rise up
against thee?

I hate them with perfect hatred: I count
them mine enemies.

Search me, O God, and know my heart:

try me, and know my thoughts:

And see if there be any wicked way in me,

and lead me in the way everlasting. (Psalm 139:1–24)

Hold on to God's Unchanging Hand and Pray!

Trust in the LORD with all thine heart; and lean not unto thine own understanding. In all thy ways acknowledge him, and he shall direct thy paths.

— P R O V E R B S   3 : 5 – 6

Prayer

Dear Father God, I will always trust in You with all my heart; I will not depend on my own understanding. I will always seek Your will in all I do, and I know that You will show me which path to take. Thank You, in Jesus's name. Amen.

Thy word have I hid in mine heart, that I might not sin against thee. (Psalm 119:11)

Prayer

Dear Father God, please help me. Please always be with me as I continue to hide Your Word in my heart so that I might not sin against You. Thank You, in Jesus's name. Amen.

> Remember now thy Creator in the days of thy youth, while the evil days come not, nor the years draw nigh, when thou shalt say, I have no pleasure in them. (Ecclesiastes 12:1)

Prayer

Dear Father God, please help me. Please don't let the excitement of my youth cause me to forget You, my Creator. Help me to honor You in my youth before I grow old and say, "Life is not pleasant anymore." Thank You, in Jesus's name. Amen.

For Your Meditation

> I will extol thee, my God, O king; and I will bless thy name for ever and ever.
> Every day will I bless thee; and I will praise thy name for ever and ever.

Great is the LORD, and greatly to be praised; and his greatness is unsearchable.

One generation shall praise thy works to another, and shall declare thy mighty acts.

I will speak of the glorious honour of thy majesty, and of thy wondrous works.

And men shall speak of the might of thy terrible acts: and I will declare thy greatness.

They shall abundantly utter the memory of thy great goodness,

and shall sing of thy righteousness.

The LORD is gracious, and full of compassion; slow to anger, and of great mercy.

The LORD is good to all: and his tender mercies are over all his works.

All thy works shall praise thee, O LORD; and thy saints shall bless thee.

They shall speak of the glory of thy kingdom, and talk of thy power;

To make known to the sons of men his mighty acts, and the glorious majesty of his kingdom.

Thy kingdom is an everlasting kingdom, and thy dominion endureth throughout all generations.

The LORD upholdeth all that fall, and raiseth up all those that be bowed down.

The eyes of all wait upon thee; and thou givest them their meat in due season.

Thou openest thine hand, and satisfiest the desire of every living thing.

The LORD is righteous in all his ways, and holy in all his works.

The LORD is nigh unto all them that call upon him, to all that call upon him in truth.

He will fulfil the desire of them that fear him: he also will hear their cry, and will save them.

The LORD preserveth all them that love him: but all the wicked will he destroy.

My mouth shall speak the praise of the LORD:

and let all flesh bless his holy name for ever and ever. (Psalm 145:1–21)

Hold on to God's Unchanging Hand and Pray!

For God so loved the world, that he gave his only begotten Son, that whosoever believeth in him should not perish, but have everlasting life. For God sent not his Son into the world to condemn the world; but that the world through him might be saved.

—JOHN 3:16–17

Prayer

Dear Father God, I thank You for loving us so much that You gave Your one and only Son, so that everyone who believes in Jesus will not perish but have eternal life. And thank You that You sent Your Son into the world not to judge the world but to save the world through Him. Thank You, in Jesus's name. Amen.

My son, forget not my law; but let thine heart keep my commandments: For length of days, and long[a] life, and peace, shall they add to thee. Let not mercy and truth forsake thee: bind them about thy neck; write them upon the table of thine heart: So shalt thou find favour and good understanding in the sight of God and man. Trust in the LORD with all thine heart; and lean not unto thine own understanding. In all thy ways acknowledge him, and he shall direct thy paths. Be not wise in thine own eyes: fear the LORD, and depart from evil. It shall be health to thy navel, and marrow to thy bones. Honour the LORD with thy substance, and with the firstfruits of all thine increase: So shall thy barns be filled with plenty, and thy presses shall burst out with new wine. My son, despise not the chastening of the LORD; neither be weary of his correction: For whom the LORD loveth he correcteth; even as a father the son in whom he delighteth. Happy is the man that findeth wisdom, and the man that getteth understanding. For the merchandise of it is better than the merchandise of silver, and the gain thereof than fine gold. She is more precious than rubies: and all the things thou canst desire are not to be compared unto her. Length of days is in her right hand; and in her left hand riches and honour. Her ways are ways of pleasantness, and all her paths are peace. She is a tree of life to them that lay hold upon her: and happy is every one that retaineth her. The LORD by wisdom hath founded the earth; by understanding hath he established the heavens. By his knowledge the depths are broken up, and the clouds drop down the dew. My son, let not them depart from thine eyes: keep sound wisdom and discretion: So shall they be life unto thy soul, and grace to thy neck. Then shalt thou walk in thy way safely, and thy foot shall not stumble. When thou liest down, thou shalt not be afraid: yea, thou shalt lie down, and thy sleep shall be sweet. Be not afraid of sudden fear, neither of the desolation of the wicked, when it cometh. For the LORD shall be thy confidence, and shall keep thy foot from being taken.

Withhold not good from them to whom it is due, when it is in the power of thine hand to do it. Say not unto thy neighbour, Go, and come again, and tomorrow I will give; when thou hast it by thee. Devise not evil against thy neighbour, seeing he dwelleth securely by thee. Strive not with a man without cause, if he have done thee no harm. Envy thou not the oppressor, and choose none of his ways. For the froward is abomination to the LORD: but his secret is with the righteous. The curse of the LORD is in the house of the wicked: but he blesseth the habitation of the just. Surely he scorneth the scorners: but he giveth grace unto the lowly. The wise shall inherit glory: but shame shall be the promotion of fools. (Proverbs 3:1–35)

Prayer

Dear Father God, I thank You for Your Word. I will never forget the things You have taught me. I will store Your commands in my heart, for if I do this, You said I will live many years and my life will be satisfying. With Your help, I will never let loyalty and kindness leave me! I will tie them around my neck as a reminder. I will write them deep within my heart. Then I will find favor with both You, O God, and people, and I will earn a good reputation. Help me to continue to trust in You with all my heart and to not depend on my own understanding. I will seek Your will in all I do, and I pray that You will show me which path to take. I won't be impressed with my own wisdom, but instead, I will fear You and turn away from evil. I pray that then I will have healing for my body and strength for my bones. I will also honor You, O God, with my wealth and with the best part of everything I produce, and I pray that then You will fill my barns with grain, and my vats will overflow with good wine. As Your child, O God, I won't reject Your discipline, and I won't be upset when You correct me. For certainly, You, O Lord, correct those You love, just as a father corrects a child in whom he delights. How joyful is the person who finds wisdom, the one who gains understanding. For wisdom is more profitable than silver, and her wages are better than gold. Wisdom is more precious than rubies; nothing I desire can compare with her. She offers me long life in her right hand, and riches and honor in her left. She will guide me down delightful paths; all her ways are satisfying. Wisdom is a tree of life to those who embrace her; happy are those who hold her tightly. By wisdom, O God, You founded the earth; by understanding, You created the heavens. By Your knowledge, the deep fountains of the earth burst forth, and the dew settles beneath the night sky. Help me to not lose sight of common sense and discernment. Help me to hang on to them, for they will refresh my soul. They are like jewels on a necklace. They keep me safe on my way, and my feet will not stumble. I praise You that I can go to bed without fear, and I will lie down and sleep soundly. And thank You that I need not be afraid of sudden disaster or the destruction that comes upon the wicked, for You, O God, are my security. I know that You will keep my foot from being caught in a trap. Help me to not withhold good from those who deserve it when it's in my power to help them. If I can help my neighbor now, please don't let me say, "Come back tomorrow, and then I'll help you." Please don't let me plot harm against my neighbor, for those who live nearby trust in me. Help me not to pick a fight without reason, when no one has done me harm. Help me not to envy violent people or copy their ways, for such wicked people are detestable to You, O God, but You offer Your friendship to the godly. Thank You, Lord, that though the curse is in the house of the wicked, certainly You bless the home of the upright. Thank You also, Lord, that though the mockers are mocked, certainly You are gracious to the humble, for the wise inherits honor, but fools are put to shame. Thank You, in Jesus's name. Amen.

To everything there is a season, and a time to every purpose under the heaven: A time to be born, and a time to die; a time to plant, and a time to pluck up that which is planted; A time to kill, and a time to heal; a time to break down, and a time to build up; A time to weep, and a time to laugh; a time to mourn, and a time to dance; A time to cast away stones, and a time to gather stones together; a time to embrace, and a time to refrain from embracing; A time to get, and a time to lose; a time to keep, and a time to cast away; A time to rend, and a time to sew; a time to keep silence, and a time to speak; A time to love, and a time to hate; a time of war, and a time of peace. (Ecclesiastes 3:1–8)

Prayer

Dear Father God, I thank You that for everything there is a season, a time for every activity under heaven. A time to be born and a time to die. A time to plant and a time to harvest. A time to kill and a time to heal. A time to tear down and a time to build up. A time to cry and a time to laugh. A time to grieve and a time to dance. A time to scatter stones and a time to gather stones. A time to embrace and a time to turn away. A time to search and a time to quit searching. A time to keep and a time to throw away. A time to tear and a time to mend. A time to be quiet and a time to speak. A time to love and a time to hate. A time for war and a time for peace. Thank You, in Jesus's name. Amen.

For Your Meditation

> Praise ye the LORD.
> Praise God in his sanctuary: praise him in the firmament of his power.
> Praise him for his mighty acts: praise him according to his excellent greatness.
> Praise him with the sound of the trumpet: praise him with the psaltery and harp.
> Praise him with the timbrel and dance: praise him with stringed instruments and organs.
> Praise him upon the loud cymbals: praise him upon the high sounding cymbals.
> Let every thing that hath breath praise the LORD.
> Praise ye the LORD. (Psalm 150:1–6)

To Share with Your Children

Give ear, O my people, to my law: incline your ears to the words of my mouth.

I will open my mouth in a parable: I will utter dark sayings of old:

Which we have heard and known, and our fathers have told us.

We will not hide them from their children, shewing to the generation to come the praises of the LORD,

and his strength, and his wonderful works that he hath done.

For he established a testimony in Jacob, and appointed a law in Israel,

which he commanded our fathers, that they should make them known to their children:

That the generation to come might know them,
even the children which should be born;
who should arise and declare them to their children:
That they might set their hope in God, and not forget the works of God,
but keep his commandments:
And might not be as their fathers, a stubborn and rebellious generation;
a generation that set not their heart aright, and whose spirit was not stedfast with God.
The children of Ephraim, being armed, and carrying bows, turned back in the day of battle.
They kept not the covenant of God, and refused to walk in his law;
And forgot his works, and his wonders that he had shewed them.
Marvelous things did he in the sight of their fathers, in the land of Egypt, in the field of Zoan.
He divided the sea, and caused them to pass through; and he made the waters to stand as an heap.
In the daytime also he led them with a cloud, and all the night with a light of fire.

He clave the rocks in the wilderness, and gave them drink as out of the great depths.

He brought streams also out of the rock, and caused waters to run down like rivers.

And they sinned yet more against him by provoking the most High in the wilderness.

And they tempted God in their heart by asking meat for their lust.

Yea, they spake against God; they said, Can God furnish a table in the wilderness?

Behold, he smote the rock, that the waters gushed out, and the streams overflowed;

can he give bread also? can he provide flesh for his people?

Therefore the LORD heard this, and was wroth:

so a fire was kindled against Jacob, and anger also came up against Israel;

Because they believed not in God, and trusted not in his salvation:

Though he had commanded the clouds from above, and opened the doors of heaven,

And had rained down manna upon them to eat, and had given them of the corn of heaven.

Man did eat angels' food: he sent them meat to the full.

He caused an east wind to blow in the heaven: and by his power he brought in the south wind.

He rained flesh also upon them as dust, and feathered fowls like as the sand of the sea:

And he let it fall in the midst of their camp, round about their habitations.

So they did eat, and were well filled: for he gave them their own desire;

They were not estranged from their lust.

But while their meat was yet in their mouths, The wrath of God came upon them,

and slew the fattest of them, and smote down the chosen men of Israel.

For all this they sinned still, and believed not for his wondrous works.

Therefore their days did he consume in vanity, and their years in trouble.

When he slew them, then they sought him: and they returned and enquired early after God.

And they remembered that God was their rock, and the high God their redeemer.

Nevertheless they did flatter him with their mouth, and they lied unto him with their tongues.

For their heart was not right with him, neither were they stedfast in his covenant.

But he, being full of compassion, forgave their iniquity, and destroyed them not: yea, many a time turned he his anger away, and did not stir up all his wrath.

For he remembered that they were but flesh; a wind that passeth away, and cometh not again.

How oft did they provoke him in the wilderness, and grieve him in the desert!

Yea, they turned back and tempted God, and limited the Holy One of Israel.

They remembered not his hand, nor the day when he delivered them from the enemy.

How he had wrought his signs in Egypt, and his wonders in the field of Zoan:

And had turned their rivers into blood; and their floods, that they could not drink.

He sent divers sorts of flies among them, which devoured them; and frogs, which destroyed them.

He gave also their increase unto the caterpiller, and their labour unto the locust.

He destroyed their vines with hail, and their sycomore trees with frost.

He gave up their cattle also to the hail, and their flocks to hot thunderbolts.

He cast upon them the fierceness of his anger, wrath, and indignation, and trouble, by sending evil angels among them.

He made a way to his anger; he spared not their soul from death,

but gave their life over to the pestilence;

And smote all the firstborn in Egypt; the chief of their strength in the tabernacles of Ham:

But made his own people to go forth like sheep, and guided them in the wilderness like a flock.

And he led them on safely, so that they feared not: but the sea overwhelmed their enemies.

And he brought them to the border of his sanctuary,

even to this mountain, which his right hand had purchased.

He cast out the heathen also before them, and divided them an inheritance by line, and made the tribes of Israel to dwell in their tents.

Yet they tempted and provoked the most high God, and kept not his testimonies:

But turned back, and dealt unfaithfully like their fathers:

they were turned aside like a deceitful bow.

For they provoked him to anger with their high places,

and moved him to jealousy with their graven images.

When God heard this, he was wroth, and greatly abhorred Israel:

So that he forsook the tabernacle of Shiloh, the tent which he placed among men;

And delivered his strength into captivity, and his glory into the enemy's hand.

He gave his people over also unto the sword; and was wroth with his inheritance.

The fire consumed their young men; and their maidens were not given to marriage.

Their priests fell by the sword; and their widows made no lamentation.

Then the Lord awaked as one out of sleep, and like a mighty man that shouteth by reason of wine.

And he smote his enemies in the hinder parts: he put them to a perpetual reproach.

Moreover he refused the tabernacle of Joseph, and chose not the tribe of Ephraim:

But chose the tribe of Judah, the mount Zion which he loved.

And he built his sanctuary like high palaces, like the earth which he hath established forever.

He chose David also his servant, and took him from the sheepfolds:

From following the ewes great with young he brought him to feed Jacob his people, and Israel his inheritance.

So he fed them according to the integrity of his heart;

and guided them by the skilfulness of his hands. (Psalm 78:1–72)

May the Lord bless and keep you.
May the Lord make His face to shine upon
you and be gracious unto you.
May the Lord lift His countenance
upon you and give you peace.
And may His peace, which passes all
understanding, keep your heart and mind,
through Christ Jesus, our Lord and only Savior.
Amen.

About the Author

Rev. Dr. Zaziiz S. L. Dinkins is the author of several books, including *Exalt Him! His Name Is JESUS!* She has served several congregations in Pennsylvania and in the New York metropolitan area as a preacher of God's holy Word. Dr. Dinkins is very active with the Exalt Jesus Ministries, which is dedicated to distributing the Word of God. She currently resides in New York, New York, with her husband and family.

Printed in the United States
By Bookmasters